SIR EDWARD BURNE-JONES

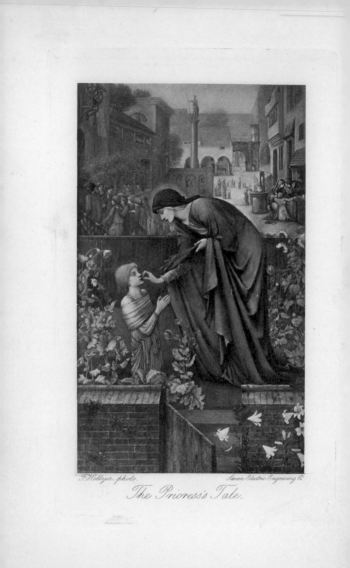

F. Hollyer, photo.   Swan Electric Engraving Co.

The Prioress's Tale.

Bell's Miniature Series of Painters

SIR EDWARD
BURNE-JONES

By MALCOLM BELL

LONDON
GEORGE BELL & SONS
1902

First Published, September, 1901.
Reprinted, November, 1901, April, 1902.

TABLE OF CONTENTS

LIST OF ILLUSTRATIONS

SIR EDWARD BURNE-JONES,
Bart.

CHAPTER I

HIS BIRTH AND EDUCATION

EDWARD BURNE-JONES was born in Birmingham on the 28th of August, 1833, of a Welsh family in no way especially distinguished, as far as can be ascertained. His great-grandfather, which is the furthest generation to which it can be traced back, is known to have been a schoolmaster at Hanbury, but his first names have been already forgotten. His only son, Edward Bevin Jones, married Edith Alvin, and had issue, a daughter Ketura, and a son Edward Richard Jones, who married Elizabeth Coley, and also had two children, a daughter Edith, and the son whose name, consolidated by a hyphen into Burne-Jones, is known throughout the civilized world.

There is no evidence to be discovered that

B

his extraordinary genius descended to him, even indirectly, from any of his forbears. His strong artistic bent would seem to be an altogether spontaneous growth, a notable one in any case, but in this one the more so as it did not burst forth until comparatively late in life. His earlier years were void of the slightest impulse towards the objects to which his later life was destined to be so utterly given up.

He went in 1844, when he was just eleven, to the old school founded in 1522 by the King Edward after whose title it is called. Here he worked diligently at the usual studies, and gained an intimate acquaintance with classic literature, together with an unusual passion for it which he nourished throughout his life. Among his class-mates were many who have also distinguished themselves in diverse ways, particularly in the Church, as witness Bishop Lightfoot and Doctor Benson, the late Archbishop of Canterbury. For this profession, indeed, Burne-Jones himself was purposing to qualify, and when in 1852 he won an exhibition which gave him the means of entering Exeter College, it was with the full intention of taking orders in due course that he went up to Oxford.

To the same college on the same day came up

another young man, also of Welsh descent, also intended for the Church, and the two fell into an acquaintanceship, destined speedily to ripen into warmest friendship, which has had an influence quite immeasurable upon the art of the last thirty years, for the young stranger thus encountered was the late William Morris.

There for the first time it was revealed to young Burne-Jones that there existed a strange enchanting world beyond the humdrum of this daily life. The first suspicion of that land of faery came to him when, in a small volume of poems by William Allingham,[1] he found a little woodcut, "Elfen Mere," signed with a curious entwinement of the initials D. G. R. This art, strange and incomprehensible as it had proved to most, found here a chord that thrilled to it in utmost sympathy. A little later and he stood in ecstasy before a more important work by the same master, and bowed himself before him. Mr. Combe, the director at that time of the Clarendon Press, was a profound admirer of the Pre-Raphaelite school, and possessed, among others, a picture by Rossetti, *Dante's Celebration of Beatrice's Birthday.*

[1] "The Music Master and other Poems," by W. Allingham (Routledge, 1855).

By this he was aroused into an enthusiasm which it were hard to over-estimate. The unknown man with the sweet-sounding foreign name who could conceive and body forth such visions became for him thenceforth a god-like hero. To paint such pictures too would be impossible, he felt, but to attempt to express even falteringly the echo that they woke within him seemed all that life was good for. By slow degrees, for all the while he was still working resolutely at his academic studies, the firm conviction grew that these were merely waste of energy, and he and Morris about the same time came to the conclusion that Art, and not the Church, was their predestinate field of action. For long he hugged the project to his breast in silence, imparting it to no one save that single friend; but in the end his longing waxed too strong for him, and he resolved to look, at least, upon the hero of his choice.

Towards the end of 1855 it was that this determination came to a head, and he set out for London to act upon it. He found out that at the College for Working Men, in Great Titchfield Street, there was an evening class for drawing to which his hero condescended to give, free of charge, some evenings every week, and thither he took his way one winter evening. He sat for some time in the glaring gas-lit room, among the new and unfamiliar company, wondering as each fresh comer passed the door, "Can that be he?" and hoping, as all fell short of his ideal, that it was not. In time a stranger, noting his solitude and manifest anxiety, came up, and, introducing himself as Mr. Vernon Lushington, drew from him the reason of his visit. He told him that Rossetti certainly would come, and promised that he should be pointed out as soon as he arrived. After a while the wistfully-watched door opened once more and there came in a man with that sweet gentle face, with its large tender eyes, high brow, and sensitive mouth shadowed by the brown moustache and beard that give the artist a look of Shakespeare in Watts's portrait of him, and Burne-Jones needed no Mentor at his side to tell him who it was. This was the hero of his dreams, and by extraordinary fortune he looked the very hero that he was. He earnestly followed him with his eyes throughout the evening, but still refused to be quite overwhelmed by the happiness of being presented to him. His new friend, Mr. Lushington, however, perceiving and humouring the mainspring of this diffidence, persuaded him to a bachelor evening at his rooms the following night, at which Rossetti had promised to be present.

With a fluttering heart he went, and shook him by the hand and spoke to him, the proudest and the happiest youth in all the city. When finally Rossetti asked him, as he asked everyone, if he too was a painter, he managed to admit that he was not, but that he longed to be, and having owned in answer to the question that he had done some drawings, was made to promise blushingly that he would bring them to the studio for consideration.

This on the whole was highly favourable, and he was urged to follow his true bent, and take at once to painting as a means of livelihood. For some time he still hesitated, "letting I dare not wait upon I would." At last he carried these, as thenceforward he carried so many difficulties and doubts, to his one hero. Rossetti questioned him as to the delay entailed by taking the degree, and when he learned that it must be, at shortest, seven months, advised him to fling the University and all its works behind him, and to set foot forthwith with firmness upon the other path. It was a hazardous counsel to give, a great responsibility to undertake, and it does marvellous credit to his perception of latent talent and scarcely full-formed character that he should dare to give and undertake with such unqualified success.

Certainly it was in no spirit of light-hearted carelessness of consequences that he exerted his new-born authority over the young man so to divert the intended course of his future life. When it was done, and Burne-Jones, with small means and with no present power to procure more, was definitely committed to his new career, Rossetti, as always while his health lasted, was lavish of encouragement of every kind.

His views upon the proper education of an artist were pronounced, and, it need not be said, entirely opposed to all the methods sanctioned by tradition. It was preposterous, he would maintain, to set a young beginner to draw straightway from the antique. You put before him, in so doing, an ideal beyond his comprehension or attainment, and either he wearies of it, or it masters him and crushes out all life and personality. You thrust on him a style in which to write before he has learned to form his letters: no wonder when the words come that they are stale and void of all vitality. Let him first learn

to express himself, however haltingly, in his own way. Let him first practise the use of his materials, and when he can avail himself of them to some good purpose, then let him go and see, as by that time he will be capable of doing, what the first masters of antiquity have done with them, in what way they have conquered obstacles with which he struggled vainly.

This is no place to argue for or against this system: rightly or wrongly it was put in action in the present case. With burning interest, mixed with a sickening sense of hopelessness, he sat day after day and followed carefully the evolution of one of those, to him, matchless masterpieces—and when the work was finished a palette and brushes were put into his hands, and he was told to paint the head of the young boy who happened to be sitting to Rossetti at the time. He was appalled at the impossibility before him, but what Rossetti said was right for him, and paint it somehow he did. The thing of horror that his production seemed to him had points that the skilled master's eye discovered, and with a hearty encouragement he bade him persevere and have no fears.

That was the whole extent of his art education, except the lessons that he gained laboriously from daily exercise of his profession carried on with indomitable resolution, and, during the earlier days, constantly overlooked and guided by Rossetti. For two years he was almost uninterruptedly in his society, and for the four or five succeeding ones he met him very frequently. His first wild hero-worship long endured, its distant awe tempered by gratitude and a sincere affection, and for a time the striking individuality of the elder man quite swept away that of the younger.

It was not until the gradual clouding of Rossetti's intellect, which darkened his later years, had so far developed, that he was no longer to be held responsible for his words or deeds, that the pain of encountering him in so sadly changed a guise became unbearable, and brought about to Burne-Jones's never failing sorrow the inevitable final parting.

Nor did Rossetti restrict his kindnesses to merely verbal counsel and applause. He got Burne-Jones an order from the proprietors of the "Illustrated London News" to do a drawing in black and white of the *Burd Helen* by the Pre-Raphaelite painter Windus, though, his capability being deemed doubtful, the order was rescinded. He also got for him the first commissions for stained-glass windows from Messrs. Powell. He introduced him to Mr. Ruskin, Mr. Arthur Hughes, and other artists, heartened him when he was depressed, and showed him many instances of his approval.

CHAPTER II

HIS PICTORIAL WORK

IN 1856, then, when he was already two years past his majority, an age at which most artists, having submitted themselves to eight or ten years of patient study, are beginning to try their strength in the arena of the public exhibitions, Burne-Jones began to draw with directed effort. As he once observed, to all intents, for the purpose of his life's work, at twenty-five he was fifteen.

Partly owing to this sense of his disabilities, partly to weakness of health at the time, much of his early work consisted of pen-and-ink drawings, carried out with extraordinary minuteness and delicacy of finish, and showing most clearly through their obvious and inevitable imperfections the passionate love of beauty, and the exquisite feeling which mark all his work from the beginning.

His very first work, *The Waxen Image*, displays, moreover, in full measure that inventiveness which was destined to become one of the leading features of the artist's creations.

The same year, 1856, witnessed his first attempt in oils, a city background to a picture illustrating the " Nibelungen Lied," a choice of subject due, perhaps, to the companionship of William Morris, who came, about that time, to share lodgings with him at 17, Red Lion Square.

The year 1857 is notable for the first of a really prodigious number of cartoons for stained glass.

In the spring of 1858 the painter who breathes so much of the spirit of Chaucer began his first direct illustration of that poet's works upon a cabinet which long stood fittingly in William Morris's drawing-room at Kelmscott House, Hammersmith Mall, and is now in the Ashmolean Museum at Oxford.

On the completion of this work he went up to Oxford to bear a part in a great scheme of decoration which owed its inception to Mr. Woodward. The Oxford Union had moved the previous year into a new building erected for it by that architect, and he suggested to Rossetti that he should paint a picture in tempera for the embellishment of a blank stretch of

wall which ran round the top of a large room
used as a library and reading-room. Rossetti
accepted the proposal with enthusiasm, and in
his busy mind it speedily developed into a much
more ambitious project. The single picture
multiplied to a whole series, and not he alone,
but all the younger artists who were in any way
under his influence were to participate. They
were to go up to Oxford in a body, living and
working all together, and in the brief passage of
a fortnight to turn the drear wall-space into a
world of beauty. Burne-Jones was persuaded to
take a part in spite of his positive and repeated
declarations that his inexperience absolutely
prohibited his undertaking a task on so large a
scale. Convinced against his will, he chose for
the subject of his contribution a legend to which
he has since returned more than once, that of
Merlin and Nimue.

This work of a fortnight extended over the
whole of that autumn and winter. The difficulties were tremendous, and were not mitigated
by Rossetti's strange preference for painting with
tempera and size directly on a thin coat of white
limewash laid upon the bare bricks.

Unfortunately, owing to the still damp con-
dition of the walls at the time and a general

ignorance among the painters of the conditions and requirements of the process employed, the results of so much toil have during the last thirty years become quite indistinguishable.

While still engaged at Oxford he occupied the intervals of the more ambitious labours in beginning a water-colour of *The Annunciation*, and during visits to Little Holland House he did drawings in pen-and-ink on vellum of *Kings' Daughters, Alice la Belle Pelerine*, from the "Mort d'Arthur," *Going to the Battle*, and *Sir Galahad*.

In September he paid a first visit to Italy, and studied the works of the great Italian masters, visiting among other places Florence, Pisa, and Siena.

On his return he settled once more in London, removing to Russell Place, Fitzroy Square. Here in the beginning of the next year, 1860, he began to paint roughly in oils the original cartoons for a window depicting sixteen incidents in the life of St. Frideswide, which were subsequently finished in 1862 and framed into a screen that adorned the artist's studio in Great Russell Street, to which he went in 1861. A pen-and-ink drawing of *Ezekiel and the Boiling Pot*, drawn in 1860 was engraved on wood by

Messrs. Dalziel for their illustrated edition of the Bible.

On June 9th the most important event in a life conspicuously uneventful apart from his art occurred when he was married in Manchester Cathedral to Miss Georgiana Macdonald.

The summer was occupied by the production of three water-colours—*Belle et Blonde et Colorée*, *Sidonia von Bork*, and *Clara von Bork*.

In the autumn a visit to the Red House, which William Morris had just built for himself at Bexley Heath, was devoted to the painting of three pictures in tempera on the walls of an upper room. The end of this year and the whole of the next two were marked by a great increase of production; but owing to the artist's method of work it is not always possible to date the individual pictures exactly. Among the earliest was an oil picture, which was afterwards reproduced, reversed, as a wood engraving, entitled *Summer Snow*, in "Good Words" for May, 1863. In the beginning of 1861 a triptych was begun as a commission from Mr. Bodley for St. Paul's Church, Brighton; but, when it was hung in the place appropriated to it in the church, the artist found that he had neglected to take due account of the distance from

which it must be regarded.   Eager, as he always
was, to profit by every lesson and to gain knowledge from his own shortcomings, he at once took
the picture back and set to work upon a second,
keeping the same composition of the Annunciation in the centre with the Magi on the wings,
but enlarging the figures, strengthening and
broadening the treatment, and substituting a
plain gold background for the more elaborate
one in the first picture.   These alterations had
the desired effect, and this amended copy now
hangs in the church.

Another of the direct realizations of subjects
from Chaucer was finished in 1861, *Cupid's
Forge*.   The original design of *Laus Veneris*
was next begun.   *The Enchantments of Nimue*
in water-colour, also painted this year, was pur-
chased in 1893 for the public by the authorities
of the Victoria and Albert Museum.

In May, 1862, Burne-Jones paid a second
visit to Italy, where he remained for three
months in the company of Mr. Ruskin, for
whom many small copies of various pictures by
the old masters were made in Venice.   On his
return *Tristram and Yseult* and *The Madness
of Tristram* were painted in water-colour.   The
water-colour *Fatima*, and a small replica of the

THE MERCIFUL KNIGHT.

same, were also painted this year. In all these later works the influence of Rossetti has perceptibly yielded by degrees to the artist's own individuality, but it revives for awhile in a little water-colour of a girl holding an apple with a scroll round it bearing the words "If hope were not, heart would break."

In 1863 Rossetti's mastery waned still further; *The Merciful Knight* and *The Wine of Circe*, which were commenced that year, show little or no traces of it. Other works of this year were two water-colours, *The Annunciation* and *The Nativity*, which were intended for Messrs. Dalziel's "Illustrated Bible," but subsequently sold by them without having been engraved for that purpose; a very charming *Cinderella*; a *St. Valentine's Day*, and the first picture in water-colour of *Green Summer*. In the course of the same year he was elected an Associate of the Royal Society of Painters in Water Colours.

Some of these works, however, were probably completed during 1864, which must otherwise have been, for no obvious reason, a singularly unproductive year.

In 1865 the artist removed to Kensington Square. A project never completed, for a large illustrated edition of William Morris's "Earthly

Paradise," was started this year, and seventy
subjects from the beautiful story of "Cupid and
Psyche" were designed.   The profound artistic
sympathy between the artist and the author
facilitated the task greatly, and rendered it a
highly congenial one to both, so much so to the
former that, the same year, he painted in water-
colour a *Zephyrus bearing away Psyche* and
Cupid finding Psyche.   This last he afterwards
repeated twice with slight alterations, and he
further re-designed the whole story for the
decoration of the Earl of Carlisle's dining-room
at Palace Green.

A set of panels of the story of *St. George* was
begun in 1865, but occupied the larger part of
the next year also before it reached completion.
It was undertaken at the request of Mr. Birket
Foster for the adornment of the dining-room in
the house at Witley to which, in conjunction
with Morris and Rossetti, he contributed so
much.   They were subsequently largely re-
painted by the artist, and in August, 1897,
gained for the painter a gold medal at the
Munich International Exhibition.

St. Theophilus and the Angel, finished this
year, shows a marked advance on all the previous
work.   Complicated groups of figures are com-

posed and handled with skill, the drawing has gained in correctness and decision, and the painter escapes finally from the direct domination of Rossetti, though the influence of that master still remains slightly perceptible.

In 1867 Burne-Jones moved to the Grange, North End Road, where another of the *Cupid and Psyche* designs was painted in water-colours. Twelve designs were made for the story of *Pygmalion and the Image*, and a water-colour in six compartments called *The Garland* was begun. Finally the first smaller version of *The Mirror of Venus* in oils was begun.

The work of the next year, 1868, was interrupted by a long illness, but a larger copy of the *Green Summer* was made in oils, and a replica of *St. Theophilus and the Angel* in water-colours, while *Flora* and the large *Chant d'Amour* were begun.

The year 1869 witnessed the completion of the *Wine of Circe* and of the first two of six water-colours—*Spring*, *Summer*, *Autumn*, and *Winter*, *Day*, and *Night*. The first of the four oil pictures of *Pygmalion and the Image*, *The Heart Desires* was next completed; then a figure of *Hymen* and a water-colour copy of *The Annunciation* for the late Dr. Radcliffe, who had shown much devoted kindness to the painter in his illness. A figure of *Rumour* was begun in water-colours, and a replica of *The Prioress's Tale*, in oils, while *Pan and Psyche* was designed.

During 1870 the water-colour of *Phyllis and Demophoön* was painted. The series begun the previous year was further enriched by *Night*. *The King's Wedding* and *Love Disguised as Reason* were other works finished this year. *Love among the Ruins, The Hesperides,* and *The Mill* were begun.

In 1871 *Summer, Day,* and *Winter* were completed. A smaller set of the *Pygmalion* pictures was begun. Another vision of *Night* ; a girl seated at an organ ; two circular pictures of singing boys and girls ; and a much altered copy of the *Chaucer's Dream*, were finished ; while *Venus Epithalamia* was painted in water-colour on canvas, and in water-colour on vellum a little picture of *The Sleeping Beauty* and *Dorigen*. This year was also in particular notable for the commencement in oil of the first small set of the now famous *Briar Rose* series, in which, however, the third picture of the Garden Court was not included.

During 1872 quite an extraordinary number of designs and pictures were begun or completed.

F. Hollyer photo].

THE WINE OF CIRCE.

Among the latter was *Fides*, and among the former *Spes*; a third companion picture was begun, *Temperantia*, and the large copy of the *Cupid and Psyche* was finished. A picture of *Danaë watching the Building of the Brazen Tower* was followed by the beginning of *Pan and Psyche* and of *Luna*, and the series from the story of *Cupid and Psyche* was arranged and drawn on canvas. Some of the designs were also painted this year and at different intervals up to 1881, but in the end the undertaking was found to be too extensive for a painter with so much other work demanding his attention, and they were finished by Mr. Walter Crane. Many designs were also made for another of Morris's poems, "Love is Enough"; much study was devoted to two designs for yet another, "The Ring given to Venus," and *The Feast of Peleus* was begun in oils. This year, in fact, was notable as the starting-point of a number of the artist's most famous works, for in addition to those already mentioned, the large *Beguiling of Merlin*, *The Angels of Creation*, and *The Golden Stairs*, were begun. The large *Chant d'Amour*, *Love among the Ruins*, and *The Hesperides*, were carried further, as was the series of *The Briar Rose*, and the triptych of *Pyramus and Thisbe* was begun.

In 1873 the artist made a brief reappearance in public at the Dudley Gallery with two pictures, *Love among the Ruins* and *The Hesperides*. *Temperantia* and *Vesper* and the *Briar Rose* series were all three finished; and *Spes*, the large *Chant d'Amour*, *The Mill*, and *St. George*, were all worked on more or less. This year also saw the beginning in oils of three celebrated works, *The Beguiling of Merlin*, the one begun the year before having been abandoned, the large *Mirror of Venus*, and *Laus Veneris*, perhaps the most discussed of the artist's exhibited works, upon which most of the year's work was spent.

The year 1874 was mainly devoted to the carrying forward of three pictures, *The Mirror of Venus*, *The Feast of Peleus*, and *Laus Veneris*; to a larger *Briar Rose* series of four pictures begun the year before, and to finishing *Pan and Psyche*.

The Beguiling of Merlin, *The Feast of Peleus*, and *Laus Veneris*, took up much of 1875, but most of it was spent in working on *The Angels of Creation*. The *Garden Court* of the *Briar Rose* series and the large *Pygmalion* set also received some attention, and *Luna* and the kneeling *Cupid* of the *Pyramus and Thisbe* triptych were finished.

The first five months of 1876 were given up
to *The Angels of Creation*, which were then
finished. A small upright picture in oils of
Danaë and the Brazen Tower was painted this
year, and *Pyramus and Thisbe*, *Hero*, and the
girls with music and viol, were finished. *The
Death of Medusa*, in the story of Perseus, was
begun, and three months were also spent upon
Perseus and Andromeda for the same series.
The Annunciation was begun, as were *The
Golden Stairs*, *The Garden of Pan*, and a small
Procession from the Romaunt of the Rose.

The year 1877 saw the opening of the Grosvenor Gallery, in time for which several works
which had been long in progress were carried
to completion.

It was, perhaps, an unprecedented event when
a painter thus displayed, practically for the first
time, to the public consideration an ample repre-
sentation of the full plenitude of his genius,
matured by long and unremitting toil. First in
perfection of design and colouring were the six
panels of *The Angels of Creation*, nearly if not
quite equalled by *The Mirror of Venus*, with
the great *Beguiling of Merlin* to complete a
noble trio of larger works, illustrating respect-
ively the symbolic, the pictorial, and the more

literary sides of the artist's development. The more Italianate and less individual personification of abstract qualities to which he has on rarer occasion given shape was seen in the companion pictures in water-colour, *Fides*, *Spes*, and *Temperantia*, while two unfinished canvases, *A Sibyl* and *A Knight*, made up this most remarkable exhibit.

Around them the war of words raged furiously. To some they were effeminate, affected, imitative, pessimistic, unwholesome, even immoral; to others full of haunting and delightful charm, masterpieces alike of drawing and of colour, the triumphant creation of a world of undreamed-of beauty, the messages of high and holy mysteries.

The public read and wondered at the conflicting comments. Too many, baffled in their expectations of a conveniently neat opinion ready cut-and-dried for daily use at ball or dinner, resigned themselves to the belief that the artist was far too profound for them, that it were vain for them to try to understand him, and that, as consolation for their wounded self-esteem, he was not worth the understanding were it possible. Had the painter, as once before, shrunk from the clamour which brawled around him and his work, and withdrawn his art thenceforth to the close transition from the easel in his studio to the chambers of his patrons, this Gallio-like indifference would in all probability have finally become the most prevailing attitude of mind. Men would have remembered for a time with wonder the dazzling meteorite that whizzed and blazed for a brief space across their narrow horizons, and then would have forgotten. This happily was not to be. The revelation of 1877 was followed by a further exposition in 1878.

For the Grosvenor Gallery of that year *Laus Veneris* was finished, and at once attracted deserved attention and applause, both for the beauty of the design and feeling, and for the resplendent glow of colouring it presented against the dull olive green of the wall on which it was hung, and a confession of delight in Burne-Jones's pictures soon ceased to be the signal for a shrug of pitying contempt. It would not, possibly, be altogether just to set down this increase of acquiescence to the well-nigh unanimous chorus of approval which rose from the French critics when, in the same year, *The Beguiling of Merlin*, by no means the finest of the painter's pictures even then, first introduced the artist to their notice at the Paris Exposition. If it were so, he would not be the only painter

to whose high deserts the eyes of English critics
have been opened by their colleagues across the
Channel. *The Mill* and *The Annunciation* and
the large *Pygmalion* pictures were worked on,
and *Atlas* and *Pegasus* for the story of Perseus,
and *Fortitude* were begun.

The earlier months of 1879 were again devoted to finishing works for the Grosvenor, and
The Story of Pygmalion and the great *Annunciation* were ready for it by May. *The Feast of
Peleus, The Hours, The Mill,* and *The Romaunt
of the Rose* designs were then taken up again,
together with *The Fortune.* In this year the
artist for the first time turned his attention to
portraiture at the request of his early and constant patron Mr. Graham, whose two daughters
he painted.

In 1880, after completing *The Golden Stairs*,
which alone represented him at the Spring Exhibition of the Grosvenor, he again devoted
himself to portraiture, painting Mr. Graham
himself. The design of *King Cophetua and the
Beggar-Maid* was projected, while a picture of
Stella Vespertina was begun, and *Cupid's Hunting Fields* was painted in low tones of grey and
green. The rest of the year was spent in preparation for the Winter Exhibition at the Gros-

venor Gallery, at which a large number of studies and designs, for the most part decorative, was shown. The most purely pictorial was *Dies Domini*.

The Grosvenor, in 1881, contained no contribution from the artist, though *The Feast of Peleus* was finished very shortly after it opened. The artist's appetite for portraits, meanwhile, seems to have grown by what it fed on, for three more were painted this year, those of *Mr. Benson*, *Lady Frances Balfour*, and *Miss Gertrude Lewis*. The *Cupid and Psyche* series in the dining-room at Palace Green received the finishing touches, and *The Wheel of Fortune*, *The Mill*, *King Cophetua and the Beggar-Maid*, and *The Hours* were worked upon at intervals. *King Arthur in Avalon* was designed and partly worked out; *The Tree of Forgiveness* and a larger *Feast of Peleus* were begun. At the annual Encænia held at Oxford in the summer, he was presented by the University with their honorary degree of D.C.L., his own college, Exeter, having before bestowed on him a fellowship. This probably was the one recognition which, among all the others that were extended to him latter, afforded him the greatest gratification.

The Wheel of Fortune was not finished for the
Grosvenor Gallery Exhibition in 1882, but *The
Mill*, together with *The Tree of Forgiveness*, two
small pictures, *The Grey Graiæ* and *Earth*, the
small *Danaë and the Brazen Tower*, *The Feast
of Peleus*, a *Study of a Child*, the sweet-faced
Angel, and the monochrome of *Cupid's Hunting
Fields* made up the artist's contribution.   The
rest of the year was mostly given to *Arthur in
Avalon*, though *The Morning of the Resurrection*
was begun, and *The Hours*, *The Flight of Perseus*, and *The Romaunt of the Rose* were carried
forwards.

In 1882 the commending voices of the French
press procured for him, in company with the
President of the Royal Academy alone, an in-
vitation from the Government to represent Great
Britain at the International Exhibition of Con-
temporary Art—a flattering request to which he
was unfortunately unable to respond.

The first months of 1883 were given to finishing the large *Wheel of Fortune* and *The Hours*,
which were exhibited at the Grosvenor together
with a portrait of *Philip Comyns Carr*, and the
smaller *Fortune* and *The Pilgrim at the Gate of
Idleness* were worked on.   Many studies were
made for *Arthur in Avalon* and *King Cophetua*

and the Beggar-Maid, and a full-sized cartoon
of the latter was drawn and coloured. The
work of the summer was grievously interrupted
by ill health, which in the autumn culminated,
and fortunately ended, in a fever. This period
of enforced relaxation was happily followed by
an access of increased vigour, which facilitated,
during the winter and the spring of 1884, the
completion of the magnificent *King Cophetua*.
This picture, exhibited with the *Wood-nymph*
at the Grosvenor the same year, assured finally
the painter's claim to the highest place in English
art. In June the subject of the *Briar Rose* was
taken up again, and the first of the series, *The
Briar Wood*, was worked on until November,
with the exception of the slight interruption
caused by the finishing of *Flora* and the painting
in July of a portrait of *Miss Fitzgerald*. In
November the painter returned to the story of
Perseus, and during the next five months produced full-sized cartoons of the last three subjects, *The Rock of Doom, The Doom Fulfilled*,
and *The Baleful Head*.

In April, 1885, he again returned to *The Briar
Wood* and finished it. The summer was devoted
to studies for *Arthur in Avalon*, and the autumn,
after the completion of the smaller *Wheel of*

Fortune, to the fourth of the *Briar Rose* pictures, *The Rose Bower*.

In 1885 the attention of the British public was finally fixed upon his importance in the art world by a demonstration, as unreliable as well may be, but the only one to which many of its members attach the least significance, the prices which his pictures fetched when put up to auction at the sale of Mr. Ellis's collection in the June of that year, prices which, though in no way sensational, betokened to the average Englishman some merit in the artist. The art that was repaid by so many guineas a square foot, he reasoned, could not but be some good—good as a speculation, haply, if in no other way; and in the same month, the Royal Academy proffered to him all unsolicited an Associateship. That this step was not followed up by the proffer of the full honours of Academicianship cannot be too much regretted, but the fact remains that it was not, and in April, 1893, the artist relieved an equivocal position by resigning his membership.

In the beginning of the following year, 1886, *The Morning of the Resurrection*, *Flamma Vestalis* and the *Sibylla Delphica* were completed and exhibited at the Grosvenor in the spring,

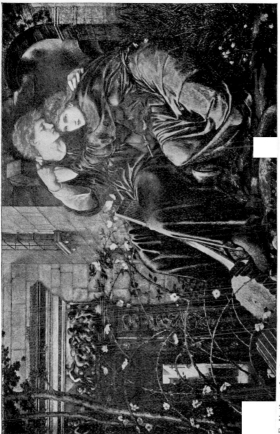

LOVE AMONG THE RUINS.

and *The Depths of the Sea*, painted on purpose, formed the only contribution which the artist ever made to the Academy.

The golden test of popularity was again applied in April, 1886, when the many works by Burne-Jones in the collection of his early and unfailing patron, the late Mr. William Graham, were sold and brought sums amounting to over seventeen thousand pounds.

The summer was spent on *The Rose Bower*, the completion of a portrait of *The Painter's Daughter*, and *The Garden of Pan*, which was finished during this winter and the spring of 1887 in time for the Grosvenor Gallery, as were *The Baleful Head*, and a portrait of *Katie*, daughter of Mrs. Lewis. Another portrait finished about the same time was that of the daughter of Professor Norton, of Harvard University.

The design for the great *Annunciation* was next worked on for awhile, and a replica made of *The Depths of the Sea*. *The Garden Court*, an *Angel*, and a *St. George*, shared the labours of the remainder of the year. *The Rock of Doom*, *The Doom Fulfilled*, and an enlarged rendering of *The Brazen Tower* were finished in the spring of 1888 and shown at the first exhibition at the

New Gallery. *The Council Room*, the second of the *Briar Rose* series, was worked on for a time, and the end of the year was spent upon two pictures, one of the *Nativity*, the other of *A King and a Shepherd*, which were finished in December for St. John's Church at Torquay, and *The Bath of Venus*, which was sent at once to the Institute at Glasgow. In 1888 he, together with Sir Frederick Burton, was unanimously re-elected a member of the Royal Society of Painters in Water Colours, from which they had both retired in 1870, in consequence of a dispute which need not be recalled.

In 1889 the Paris Exhibition showed further the estimation in which foreign critics held him, and brought him the ribbon of the Knight of the Legion of Honour. *The Star of Bethlehem* was begun, but nearly the whole of this year and the early part of 1890 were spent in finishing the magnificent *Briar Rose* series, which were bought by Messrs. Agnew and exhibited during the summer to crowds of visitors.

The rest of the year and the spring of 1891 were given to *The Star of Bethlehem* and *Sponsa di Libano*, which were both finished and exhibited at the New Gallery that year.

A long and painful illness now unhappily

intervened to stay the painter's hand, and it was not until the spring of 1892 that he was well enough to resume work upon the earlier *Briar Rose* series in oils, and *The Sirens.* The large design of *The Annunciation* for the American Church at Rome was produced this year and sent to the Murano Glass Company for execution in mosaic. *The Pilgrim at the Gate of Idleness* and *The Heart of the Rose* were next taken up and completed for the New Gallery in 1893, and the large *Perseus and the Graiæ* was also finished about the same time and exhibited at the Salon in the Champ de Mars, Paris. A design for *The Tree of Life*, also executed in mosaic, was carried out, and a portrait of *Miss Gaskell* painted this year, but most of it was given up to a reproduction in oils of *Love among the Ruins.* These were exhibited at the New Gallery in 1894, together with *Vespertina Quies.* The jury at the Exhibition at Antwerp awarded him a first class medal, and in February that year Queen Victoria conferred upon him the honour of a baronetcy. The year was devoted to advancing several works, among which *The Fall of Lucifer*, a delightful portrait of *Miss Dorothy Drew*, the first version of the fourth of the *Briar Rose* series, and *The Wed-*

D

ding of Psyche were ready for the New Gallery in
1895. In 1896 his contributions to the New
Gallery were *Aurora* and *The Dream of Launcelot
at the Chapel of the San Graal*, while the winter
exhibition of the Water-colour Society included
some studies. The New Gallery in 1897 contained only one of the artist's pictures, *The
Pilgrim of Love*. Much time was subsequently
given to work on *Arthur in Avalon* and to the
completion of *The Prioress's Tale*, and a figure of
St. George, which were sent to the New Gallery
in 1898.

Ill health more than once, unhappily, interrupted the labours of the succeeding year,
and especially an attack of influenza in the
early months. From this, however, he had ap-
parently quite recovered, when shortly after mid-
night of June 16th he was taken suddenly ill,
and in the early morning of June 17th passed
away. The preceding day had been passed in
the quiet content of his studio, and there was no
premonition that the hand that laid down the
brush at twilight would never take it up again.
Spared the lingering weariness of illness, and
the sad conviction of failing skill, in the full
plenitude of his powers he was called swiftly
and—for him—mercifully away, leaving much

unaccomplished by which the world would have been richer, but leaving, nevertheless, such a legacy of perfected beauty as has seldom, if ever, been equalled.

CHAPTER III

HIS DECORATIVE WORK

REMARKABLE both for its quantity and quality as Sir Edward Burne-Jones's pictorial work is, and frequent as have been the opportunities given to the public for forming an opinion of it, he is to this day, as I imagine, more widely and more favourably known by his still more numerous productions of a decorative character.

Works of such price as this artist's pictures inevitably fell into the hands of private patrons, and after their first appearance in a public gallery, if even they attained to that, were caught away from the general eye only to emerge again occasionally, at uncertain intervals and for a brief space, while other patrons dispute at Christie's the right of future guardianship.

Decorative art, on the other hand, is largely popular and democratic. Much decorative work, of course, contributes to the adornment of private houses, but a large remainder becomes, as far as free enjoyment of it goes, the property of all, and counts its admirers by tens of thousands while the picture reckons only hundreds.

Another reason for this wider field of influence occupied by works of a decorative nature is to be found in the conditions of their manufacture. In pictorial work of this elaborate nature the details must be carried out by the artist's own hand, whereas in decorative work the execution may be intrusted, in large part at all events, to less skilful workmen whose time is of less value.

In this last point the designer was particularly fortunate, since he found in William Morris a mind in singular affinity with his own, and in the craftsmen trained under his control hands admirably adapted to carry to the utmost pitch of excellence any idea that he might indicate.

It is in this perfect sympathy of aim and method between the two that we discover the reason of the mighty force that they exerted over the domestic art of the last thirty years.

Almost the first works that he produced were cartoons for stained-glass windows, drawn and coloured in 1857, for Messrs. Powell of Whitefriars. Three of these cartoons were executed,

Adam and Eve, The Tower of Babel, and *King Solomon and the Queen of Sheba,* and are now in the dining hall of St. Andrew's College, Bradfield, Berkshire. Another work, designed also for the same firm, was the St. Frideswide window in Christ Church, Oxford, which was executed in 1859. A great window of *The Creation* for Waltham Abbey, designed in 1861, was the last work done for Messrs Powell. Thenceforth in the production of stained-glass windows the names of Burne-Jones and William Morris are inseparably associated.

Various and numberless, in fact, as the results of their co-operation have been since Morris began the business which was destined to reform the taste of England, they are seen most conspicuously in the stupendous catalogue of stained-glass windows, designed for him by this artist, and executed by him and his workmen. It seems incredible that one man could have produced so much, and it is only when one knows with what extraordinary speed and certainty the artist worked out the cartoons, that the apparent impossibility vanishes, to leave behind it a growing wonder at the precision of eye and hand, which never hesitated, the wonderful fertility of invention, which never failed, and the profound knowledge of form and fold ever ready to be drawn upon for details of every kind.

Words, however, must fail utterly to describe the differing schemes of colour employed, some glowing with the brilliant hues of gems, others delicate variations of but three or four tints. The contrast between the two cannot be seen to better advantage anywhere than at Christ Church, Oxford, where the archway at the entrance to the choir is flanked on each side by a specimen of either style, the *St. Frideswide* window almost dazzling in its splendour, and the enchanting *St. Cecilia* window.

To enter into the consideration of the details of even a tithe of these designs would lead us far beyond the limits of space available. Three only may be mentioned for reasons apart from their artistic value. The magnificent window in Holy Trinity Church, Sloane Street, is the most important of the few easily accessible to Londoners. That in Hawarden Church was intended as a memorial of the Right Honourable W. E. Gladstone's long connection with that parish, but before the window was entirely in place death had severed the tie, and it was not unveiled until after the dead statesman had been interred in Westminster Abbey. Lastly, in the mellow light cast by the windows in the quiet country church at Rottingdean, on the afternoon of June 21st, 1898, the funeral service of the great artist was conducted, and in the sunny south-west angle, just without, his ashes repose, ringed round by flowering red and white valerian.

The works in stained glass have been mentioned to begin with, because that was the first form in which the artist's decorative faculties found expression, and because the examples of it are by far the most numerous and widely distributed. The splendid achievement next to be considered is, however, in every way the most important decorative scheme to which he has given shape, and is, in all human probability, the work by which this painter will longest survive the chances and changes of destroying time. Ghirlandajo is reported to have said that he alone designed for eternity who worked in mosaic, and it is in that enduring and resplendent material that Burne-Jones has written his name for all posterity to read. In 1882 the chance came to him to decorate the American Protestant Church which had been built by Mr. Street, the English architect, in the Via Nazionale at Rome.

The cartoons of *The New Jerusalem* were begun in 1883, and finished and sent to Doctor

Salviati's glass works at Murano for execution before the end of 1884. The original scheme comprised a large series of mosaics, and in the succeeding years further designs of *The Fall of the Rebel Angels*, *The Tree of Life*, *The Annunciation*, and other similar subjects were made.

To measure year by year the flood of beauty that he poured into the world would be a serious undertaking; merely to indicate the most important and typical details is all that can be attempted here. There is scarcely a single department of the Applied Arts in which the artist did not at one time or another labour, either directly or in designs to be carried out by Morris or other skilled workers. Many of his pictures were intended to form a part of schemes for wall decoration; he designed several bas-reliefs, and himself executed others in gesso; both the piano and the organ have been embellished by his hand, while one of his earliest works in oil was on a cabinet: tapestry, and needlework, and woven stuffs have claimed his attention; a number of tiles in Mr. Birket Foster's former house at Witley owe their great beauty to him; a form of bas-relief in which metal, woodwork, and gesso are variously stained, gilded, and glazed, is an invention of his own; he guided the hand of the goldsmith and set forth *The Triumph of Love* upon the frail surface of a fan ; and, finally, he worked incessantly from the beginning of his career at cartoons for stained-glass windows.

CHAPTER IV

SOME FEATURES OF HIS ART

IN delivering his first lecture to the young students placed under his charge on the opening of the Slade School of Fine Arts at University College, London, in October, 1871, Mr. E. J. Poynter, R.A., said: "Remember that the true object of art is to create a world, not to imitate what is constantly before our eyes."

This remark, which should be inscribed in letters of gold round the rim of every art-critic's ink-pot, made by so scholarly and earnest a painter on an occasion on which he would naturally weigh, with more than usual care, the truth and meaning of his words, would deserve a full and instantaneous acceptance, even were it not supported by a number of similar utterances by other artists of skill.

Another Slade professor, Mr. Sidney Colvin, of Cambridge, has said: "What reasonable judges require of an artist, and especially of an imaginative artist, is not that his work should conform to their own standard, but that it should be good of its kind, and that its kind should be personal to himself."

Armed with these two axioms, and using them honestly and sincerely, the student will be in a position to judge fairly the painter's work. They will not, of course, insure that he shall like it, for it displays so constant and powerful an individuality, that it must either win or revolt his sympathy, but they will prevent him from trying it with false standards ; they should show him that, whether he likes or dislikes it, it is in itself excellent and worthy of all respect, and they ought to hinder his falling in with the fallacies of some of the critics who have so furiously attacked the artist.

Two strange errors have obscured the minds of some of his really critical assessors. Firstly, the conviction that his art is "not the outcome or even a generalization of nature." It is a frequent assumption that he painted to a large extent "out of his head," without considering or observing nature, an assumption which is the more remarkable as a long series of his studies in various materials have been on exhibition at various times. The many reproductions of

F. Holyer photo.]

THE MIRROR OF VENUS.

such studies which have been published of late years show with what minute particularity, what staunch fidelity he followed nature. Hands and faces, feet and figures, flowers and foliage, every wrinkle of a robe, every twist of a scarf, every feather of a wing, the complicated plaitings of a headdress, the curves and angles of armour, the folds and creases of a baby's limbs, were painstakingly noted and set down. It is not too much to say that scarcely a square inch of any one of his canvases has not been the outcome of devoted care, as for example, the little figures of Adam and Eve which stand in the globe of the sixth angel of creation, and which were as carefully studied from the life as though they were to be painted of full size.

No painter went more constantly or reverently to nature, but he did not consider that to copy her slavishly was the be-all and end-all of art. He used nature, not abused her, and like Turner he learned from her in order that he might utilize his knowledge, and not merely make an inventory of it and show men that he had it. He blended and transmuted her gifts in a way of his own which is of nature, yet above it. One might transfer to him with equal justice a pithy question put by Turner to a critic who complained that he never saw in nature such skies as his. "No," said the artist, "but don't you wish you could?"

Secondly, that the weaknesses and inconsistencies of his earlier technique, the result of the system of his education as initiated by Rossetti, were wilfully assumed in imitation of certain unidentified early Italian painters who were also imitated by the Pre-Raphaelite Brethren. Faults of drawing, recognizable by the veriest ignoramus, are, of course, to be found in all his earlier works; but they are accidental, not intentional, and there is in spite of them an all-pervading sense of beauty and delicacy of feeling about these tentative efforts at self-expression.

The sources of inspiration from which he drew many of his subjects are highly interesting as illustrating phases in his development, and in throwing light upon the real origin of that Italianized spirit that many profess to detect in his works. In the earlier days, while he was still under the influence of Rossetti, the "Mort d'Arthur" and certain of the less known Border Ballads strongly affected his imagination, and several of the works of this period are derived from these, as *The Beguilements of Nimue, The Madness of Tristram, Sir Degrevant, Clerk*

Saunders, and much more recently, *King Co-phetua and the Beggar-Maid*; but the author who first captured his fancy and held it longest was "the well of English undefiled," the poet Chaucer.

His first oil-painting was suggested by the Prioress's Tale; the "Assembly of Foules" prompted several water-colours, and a large number of designs drawn at various times from "The Romaunt of the Rose" and "The Legende of Goode Women." It is, however, for its general effect upon all his work rather than for the direct realizations it has inspired, that this fascination is most remarkable, since we can, I believe, trace clearly to it the sentiment that is, as a rule, attributed to an assimilation with the early Italian painters. Italian, indeed, it remains, but far more remotely. Chaucer himself borrowed largely from Boccaccio, and still more from the authors of the old French metrical romances, who in their turn took their good where they found it among the Italian poets. His allegories were Chaucerian, with the single exception of the *Mask of Cupid*, which comes from later Italy through Spenser.

The artist shared with Chaucer his passionate love of birds and flowers, and lavished them with

a tender hand over his work; in especial, like the
poet, he delighted in the English flower, the rose.
It veils the desolation of his ruins, it heightens
the beauty of his gardens, it crowns his Cupid,
and drops in the pathway of his Goddess of Love,
and his great work, *The Legend of the Briar
Rose*, is quite an apotheosis of the beloved flower.
His season, like Chaucer's, was ever May, a time
of song and blossoming, but one also, like the
poet's, the merriment of which was almost entirely limited to nature, for the spirit of sadness
that breathes from Burne-Jones's pictures is
Chaucer's.

" A manner ease, medled with grevaunce," [1]
and "lustie thoughts fulle of great longinge" is
the frame of mind of almost all his men and
maidens. In the lovely girls clustered around
the Venus' mirror we find it, and still more
in the knight and lady in the *Chant d'Amour*
and the pensive princess in *Laus Veneris*. It
looks out at us from the eyes of the man and
woman in *The Garden of Pan*, and in *Love
among the Ruins* it weighs like lead upon the
persecuted Psyche; even the *Sponsa di Libano* is
infected with it. It is the sadness, the bitterness
of love that predominates in the merrie month.

[1] Chaucer's " Cuckoo and Nightingale."

TEMPERANTIA.

His landscapes are the dream-lands in which Chaucer wandered, of the earth, yet not earthly. He, too, liked to adorn his imaginings with a wealth of colour and decoration, embroidery and jewelry, pictured tapestries, carvings in wood and marble, painting and goldsmith's work, and he, too, sought to give them significance as well as beauty.

His classical figures, with their surroundings, are such as Chaucer imaged them, his Troy is that of Dares Phrygius and Dictys Cretensis, not of Homer or Virgil. Take, for example, the beautiful *Feast of Peleus*.

It is an enchanting little picture, radiant with colour, but it is not classical, nor is it Italian. These are the half-Pagan, half-Christianized deities of Chaucer, Dan Cupido and his mother Saint Venus ; Pluto, "the king of faycrye," who quotes Salomon and Ecclesiasticus, and Proserpine, who cites the Christian martyrs and the "Gesta Romanorum."

When the artist left Chaucer himself, it was very often only to find him again under a more modern guise in the works of "the idle singer of an empty day."

All the story of Perseus, and that of Cupid and Psyche, are presented in the mediæval man-

E

ner in which Morris saw them. *The Brazen Tower* is his in spirit, translated into form and colour by the painter.

The four pictures from *The Story of Pygmalion*, also included in "The Earthly Paradise," again show this preference of the poet and the artist for the spirit before the form, provided only the last be beautiful.

Among the pictures drawn from the last of the artist's literary sources, the Bible, we might expect to find traces, if anywhere, of the Italian masters, and in some of the earliest works we do. There is a curious water-colour triptych, painted in 1862-63, soon after the artist's return from his second visit to Italy, which shows an evident desire to reproduce the peculiar naïveté of the Sienese school.

The scarlet-hung bedstead and other accessories in *The Annunciation* painted in 1861-62 also show obvious suggestions of the Italian, but a sweeping charge of imitation can scarcely rest on such slight grounds as these two works.

That these, moreover, were the result of an isolated impulse on the painter's part, not of a persistent effort, or even of an irresistible influence exercised over him by the school he chose once or twice to imitate, is evident if we glance for a moment at the other works begun or finished about the same time, as for instance, *The Wine of Circe*, *The Merciful Knight*, *Cinderella*, or *Green Summer*, in none of which is there a sign of imitation.

Nor, turning to the third division of the artist's works, the symbolical, which includes all personifications of abstract qualities or natural phenomena, do we find more evidence of the supposed Italian imitation, though we might well look for it there. *The Angels of Creation*, *Venus*, *Concordia*, and *Venus Discordia*, the *Hours*, and the *Seasons*, *Day*, and *Night*, *Earth*, *Luna*, and *Flora*, are all distinctively individual, and though the idea of *The Wheel of Fortune* is an often used one, the vision of it which the painter shows us, the impassive careless goddess and the submissive victims of her caprice, are distinctly modern and original.

In one point alone did he approximate more nearly than other English painters to the art of early Italy. He cared not at all for minute archæological accuracy. That the garments and accessories should be in themselves beautiful and susceptible of rich adornment and fine colouring, that they should be subordinate to and yet expressive of, the spirit of the picture, outweighed in his eyes all such considerations as whether the person represented would really have worn such clothes in such surroundings. It was the soul that he strove after, and so long as the mantle that enwraps it was seemly and pleasing to the eye, he asked no more.

We see this in all his work, decorative and pictorial. The wily *Vivien*, weaving her mystic paces among the flowering hawthorn trees, could not, perhaps, have known that weird clinging dress with its purple shadows and steely lights, but it is a delight to look upon, and its sinister strangeness is truly significant of the cunning traitress. His *Fatima* has little characteristically eastern in her garments. There is a suggestion of a turban in the ring-like headdress crowning her waving locks, but there is no certain place or period for the big swelling sleeves, the V-shaped bodice with its embroidered hearts, or the long folds of the skirt; yet the feeling of anxiety and expectation, of mystery and danger, is wonderful, and the veriest child, who had once heard the tale, would recognize its heroine in this lovely figure.

To the Magi, in *The Star of Bethlehem*, he gave a more oriental aspect, but it is merely in broad suggestions, not in petty precisions. The first grey-headed king wears a scarf bound turban-wise about his helmet, but no Asiatic monarch ever wore such a crown as he has laid humbly down among the blossomed herbage at the feet of the grave-faced Virgin. The earnest youth behind him bears armour which Meyrick himself would find it hard to date, and the adoring negro prince has on his mantle embroideries which only western nuns could have stitched in the dim silences of mediæval convents. Yet, individually and collectively, they are all exquisite, and the self-abasement of wealth and power before the weak majesty of a homeless mother and her babe has never found a truer or a fairer exposition.

The ingenious gentleman who writes annually to point out the botanical and zoological errors of unscientific artists had no terrors for him. What matters it that Circe, enchantress though she was, would not be likely to have changed her victims into a species of cat unknown to the old world, or to adorn her chamber with sunflowers as yet growing unrevealed to Europe on the broad prairies of America? The black panther is more malevolently feline in appearance than his Asiatic cousins, and there is a suggestion of bale and bane in the strong black and

yellow of the innocent sunflower that assists in
conveying the sentiment of the work, of embody-
ing the idea in the painter's mind, and that was
all-sufficient for him.   It seems mere pedantry
in the face of it to maintain that Circe, if she
had ever wrought her spells, could not have
done so under such conditions.

In his decorative work we do see many instances of skilful adaptation of Italian methods,
for he was too sound an artist not to know when
the best cannot be bettered, though here also
it is chiefly marked by the same determinate
disregard of little accuracies.   This is perhaps
most notable and has been most observed in the
grand window of *The Building of the Temple*, in
Trinity Church, Boston, which city shares with
New York, Albany, Longwood, and Newport,
the honour of being pioneers in American ap-
preciation of this artist.

In such a work strict adherence to fact, even
if it were possible, is quite uncalled for.   The
artist has not affected even to desire it.   The
dresses of the aged councillors are, indeed,
oriental in general character, but the armour of
the king and his attendant knights is frankly
mediæval in design, and the throne and its canopy
as undisguisedly Byzantine.   That King David

never did wear such a suit of mail or sit on such
a throne it needs no scholar to declare, but an
attempt at re-creating an approach to what he
might have used, would possibly have resulted
in but little nearer approach to the unknown
truth, and would most certainly have lacked the
decorative qualities at present found in the production.

In one other point, moreover, the painter did
follow closely the early Italian painters, one in
which he might well find fellow-imitators, namely
the tireless attention he paid to his craft, as an
important part of his art.   Hasty or careless work
he never once produced, while he spared no
pains to insure that the materials he employed
should be sound and enduring.   With all his
devotion to art and the lofty views he took of it,
he never permitted himself to forget that the
painting of a picture is in essence a manufacture, and that sound workmanship is as necessary
a part of it as of a chair or table.   His pictures
were built up with as much thought for their
endurance as well as for the beauty of their
general effect and appropriateness of detail as a
Gothic cathedral.   The permanence of a colour
was to him as serious a matter as the strength of
his stone or timber to the architect, and as a

consequence the beautiful *Green Summer*, to choose an example haphazard from all his works, is as fresh and bright in appearance to-day as when it left the artist's easel in 1868.

His first process in the creation of a picture was the crystallization of the floating visions in his mind into a design carefully drawn out in chalk or pencil. This was generally modified from time to time, while numerous studies for every detail were carried out in the intervals of other work. In the case of a large picture this was, as a rule, followed by a cartoon painted in water-colours of the same size as the proposed canvas, and finished elaborately from a small coloured sketch. From this the final work was copied, and further studies were made before the painting was begun. Each stage of this was left to dry thoroughly, often for months at a time, before another was commenced, and when the last had been concluded, the whole was left for several years before it was permitted to be varnished, an operation which he always preferred to perform himself with scrupulous care.

Thus, in conclusion, we find in the production of each individual work this same inexhaustible patience, unfailing honesty of purpose, and minute care for the smallest details, which, ceaselessly exercised for forty-three years, raised the young artist of 1856, blindly groping in the footsteps of a masterful leader, into the most original and distinctive painter that England has produced, whose fame has spread from among a small circle of staunch admirers out to the furthermost borders of the world of Art. In France it stands amongst the highest. There many cordial acknowledgments were supplemented some years ago by the election of Burne-Jones to a Corresponding Membership in the Department of Painting in the Academy of Fine Arts in France, an honour which seems likely to be followed by his unsought promotion to leadership among the younger generation of artists who are in revolt alike against the formalism of the Academy and the emptiness of realism and impressionism.

Useful as his influence may be as an inspiring motive to the young Parisian painters, it is to be hoped that they will not attempt the impossible, an effort to imitate his style, the originality and individuality of which are necessarily unattainable. It is because each picture of his was an expression of himself that his peculiar genius is inimitable. It is this personal element that is to his admirers so irresistibly attractive.

CHAPTER V

OUR ILLUSTRATIONS

SIR EDWARD BURNE-JONES'S pictures lend themselves less than those of most artists to a division into periods. We can discover in them neither a sudden and radical change of method, such as, for instance, denoted Sir John Millais' secession from the Pre-Raphaelite brotherhood, nor a marked transfer of interest from one class of subjects to another, such as may be observed in the works of Sir L. Alma-Tadema, Sir E. J. Poynter and others. Having chosen his path he never swerved from it, and the works left unfinished at his death differ only from those of 1856 in the greater perfection of their technical means.

Nor would it be any advantage to divide them into oil and water-colour pictures, for he made little or no distinction between the two materials; his technical methods of using both were practically identical, and it would be impossible to

DANAË AND THE BRAZEN TOWER.

say in any given case why he had chosen one material rather than the other.

They can, however, be conveniently arranged in classes according to the source of inspiration from which the subject was drawn, and our illustrations have accordingly been selected with a view to giving as typical a representative as possible of each class. These, some of which have already been considered, are seven in number I.—Those chiefly dating from the period of Rossetti's greatest influence suggested by mediæval ballads or legends. II.—Those taken from the classics. III.—Those inspired by William Morris's series of poetical stories "The Earthly Paradise." IV.—Those due to Chaucer. V.—Subjects drawn from the Bible. VI.—Allegorical subjects. And VII.—Works of pure imagination. The order in which these classes are here set out is it may be added, purely arbitrary, since they have in themselves no chronological significance no one for any length of time having absorbed his energy to the exclusion of the rest, and we shall therefore, in proceeding to consider the pictures, do so in order of their inception as far as ascertainable.

The Prioress's Tale (see *frontispiece*) is cer-

tainly the first in this respect, though it was as a
matter of fact the last picture that he finished.
This curious circumstance was due to the persist-
ency of his ideas, reacting with his methods of
work. A conception once formed in his mind was
rarely abandoned or wearied of. A picture designed one year might not be begun till ten years
later, might not be completed for another ten or
more, but his interest in his subject never failed
him, and his comprehension of exactly what he
meant to do with it was as distinct and as
unaltered at the last as at the first. However
long the lapse of time might be, when he
returned to it, he did so with as vivid a recollec-
tion of what he had intended as though he had
but laid it aside at dusk the day before. He
kept in this way a large number of pictures in
a state of progress or of suspended animation,
working at each only when in the mood, and
laying it aside for some other at frequent intervals, until the moment seemed ripe for its
completion, though even then he nearly always
preferred to finish more than one about the
same time.

Of this deliberate method the present work is
a notable example. It was first designed in
1858, and painted in oils as part of the decora-

tion of a cabinet, which was for many years in the possession of Morris, and is now in the Ashmolean Museum at Oxford. The picture itself was not begun until eleven years later in 1869, and only finished in 1898, when it formed part of the last contribution he ever sent to the New Gallery. The subject, belonging to Class IV., is taken from Chaucer, illustrating the story told by the Prioress on the road to Canterbury, of the little "Christen" child who angered the Jews of a "great citee in Acy" by singing the praises of the Virgin on his way through the Jewry to school, and who was consequently waylaid and murdered by an assassin hired by them. His mother, seeking him and calling him by name, passed near the place where his body with the throat cut lay in a dark cupboard, and straightway he began to sing "Alma Redemptoris," and so continued, even after his murderers had been captured and he had been laid on his bier before the high altar, until the abbot asked him why he sang so. The boy replied that the Virgin had laid a grain beneath his tongue, by virtue of which he retained consciousness and was enabled to continue chanting her praises until it was removed. The abbot thereupon took out the grain and the child died. In treating the subject Burne-Jones has eliminated the horror, adapting rather than directly illustrating the story. The scene, instead of the loathsome wardrobe of Chaucer's tale, is a narrow grass-grown graveyard set with poppies and sunflowers, and the cut throat, which is so insisted on in the story, is ignored, the boy's death being indicated by his pale face, closed eyes, and bound arms. The Virgin, in a long blue mantle falling in stately folds, stoops towards him, about to place in his mouth the grain which she has just taken from a bunch of ears held in her left hand. In the background is the Jewry, in no way Asiatic, but frankly medi-æval English, as doubtless Chaucer himself saw it in his mind's eye, and here, by a device borrowed from the early masters, two other earlier scenes from the story are depicted. On the left the boys are going into the school, on the right a woman with a knife in her left hand draws to her the boy who kneels at her feet while a man leaning from a shop urges her to the murder. The beauty of the picture lies partly, as in all Burne-Jones's works, in the rich and splendid colouring, partly in the tender and restrained sentiment, partly in the wealth of careful detail, the quaint picturesqueness of the city background, the sweet dignity of the Virgin, the stiff pathetic little figure of the boy, and the exquisite treatment of the plants, the wall-flowers on the red-brick wall, the poppies and sunflowers, and the white lilies of the Madonna in the foreground. Every inch of the picture is full of charm, and worth a careful study.

Our second picture, *The Merciful Knight* (p. 16), was finished in 1863, though it was certainly begun some years earlier, as we know by a story connected with it. Rossetti early in his acquaintance with Burne-Jones gave to him a number of his drawings and designs for purposes of study, and Burne-Jones treasured them as the apple of his eye. One day some few months later Rossetti came to see him, and found him painting on the background of this very picture. He stood for some time watching in silence, and then abruptly asked him for the studies he had formerly given him, and on receiving them, without a word, tore them into fragments and went away, meaning thereby that Burne-Jones had nothing more to learn from him. And indeed this peaceful woodland landscape seen against the sun is exquisite enough to justify his conclusion. The story of the picture, which belongs to Class I., is told by an inscription on the frame "of a knight who forgave his enemy when he might have destroyed him; and how the image of Christ kissed him in token that his acts had pleased God." In this again we have to observe the varied beauty of the accessories, the woodwork and decoration of the shrine, the armour of the knight, the marigolds in the grass, the roses on the wattle fence, but always in the end we come back to the landscape with its sunlit pool and wooded hillside, perhaps the most truthful, certainly the most beautiful, among many true and beautiful.

The Wine of Circe (p. 20), taken from the classics, was begun in 1863 and finished in 1869. The story of Circe whose wine-cup turned all men who partook of it into beasts is too well known to need retelling, and we need do no more than point out how subtly each detail, beautiful in itself, conduces to the feeling of threatening evil, the pale dark-haired witch in her orange robe crouching malevolently with outstretched snake-like arm, the steel throne and dragon-twined tripod, the heavy black and orange sunflowers, the inky panthers with their wicked yellow eyes, and the thick blood-like

gouts of the deep purple potion she is adding
drop by drop to the wine-jar in preparation for
the mariners whose broad-sailed vessels are seen
through the window hastening over the sunlit
sea.

The fourth and fifth belong to Class VII.,
works of pure imagination, in which naturally
enough the most characteristic works of the artist are to be found. The original *Love among the
Ruins* (p. 30) was begun in 1870 and finished in
1873, but this, in 1893, was hopelessly damaged
by the blundering of a photographer in Paris,
and the existing picture is a replica painted
soon afterwards for the owner of the first. It is
one of the most intense and significant of the
artist's works, and can only be compared in its
effect upon the mind with a strain of sweet sad
music, hackneyed as such a comparison must
seem. There is no story. It is just a realization
of the triumph of love over worldly ruin, con-
veyed with consummate mastery, and notable in
particular for the admirable composition of the
two figures and the haunting expressions of the
faces. This may, indeed, be almost regarded as
a test-case among Burne-Jones's pictures, for to
those to whom this does not appeal he can have

F

nothing to say, however much the mere beauty of others of his works may please them.

The Mirror of Venus (p. 44) was begun on a small scale in 1867, and a second larger one in 1873, while both were finished in 1877, and are in many ways the most purely beautiful of all his creations.   The idea itself of Venus first introducing femininity to the fascinations of the mirror in the shape of a glassy pool is charming, and the carrying of it out is no less exquisite.   The grace of the various girlish figures, sitting, kneeling, or standing about the water, can be fully appreciated, even in a reproduction in black and white, but no words can do justice to the varied harmony of the glowing colour.   Especially to be noted in the picture itself are the flowers which he loved and studied so fondly, the broad water-lily leaves, the sheets of blue forget-me-nots, and the white flowered myrtle beside the tall blue-clad Venus. Notable also are the different attitudes of the girls, some gazing at themselves in wonder, others absorbed in frank self-admiration, while two alone turn from their own attractions to gaze in awe upon the far greater beauty of the goddess.

Temperantia (p. 48) is one of many allegorical

subjects included in Class VI., and the symbolism
of the stately woman pouring water from a jar
on to the flames which are powerless to harm
her own bare feet is too simple to need com-
ment. It was begun in 1872 and finished in
the following year.

Danaë and the Brazen Tower (p. 58), which
was painted in 1888, though derived originally
from the classics, belongs rather to those subjects forming Class III., the direct inspiration of
which came from "The Earthly Paradise," and
which may be best described in Morris's own
words, "Acrisius, King of Argos, being warned
by an oracle that the son of his daughter Danaë
should slay him, shut her up in a brazen tower
built for that end beside the sea." As Morris
imagined it and as Burne-Jones painted it,
Danaë was ignorant of what an evil bearing on
her destiny the tower was to have, and watched
its building with innocent wonder alone. The
picture is one of those compositions in vertical
straight lines which he more than once produced.
Notice the tall, narrow portal, with the heavy iron-
studded door on the right; in the foreground
the straight stems of iris and columbine; in the
background, beyond a rough-paved courtyard

inclosing a tank, the straight sides of the circular
brazen tower, the corner of a stone one, the
narrow arcades and lofty turrets of the town, the
poles and ladder of the scaffolding, the stern
figure of King Acrisius surrounded by armed
guards and counsellors, and the labourers, one
alone of whom stoops into a curve to reach
the mortar at his feet; within the garden the
irregular spire of a cypress tree, against which
stands Danaë gathering her cloak about her into
stately perpendicular folds with one hand, while
with her chin resting upon the other she gazes
wonderingly at the strange work in progress.

The Star of Bethlehem, one of his Biblical
subjects, is a large water-colour, which is a reproduction, slightly altered, and that chiefly in the
colour scheme and the more strictly pictorial
treatment of details, of the tapestry designed by
the artist and executed by William Morris for
Exeter College, Oxford. The outcome of a
commission offered by the Corporation of
Birmingham in 1887, it was begun in the
autumn of 1888 and finished in the spring of
1891. There is nothing, as indeed there is no
room for anything, particularly novel in the
treatment of the subject, if we except the intro-

Caswall Smith *photo.*] [*by permission of the Corporation of Birmingham.*

THE STAR OF BETHLEHEM.

luction of the hovering angel bearing the guid-
ing star, which we do not remember in any
other treatment of the story. The deliberate
ignoring of archæological accuracy has already
been referred to, and as this is fortunately one
of the too few works of the master accessible at
all times to the public, while it lends itself
unusually well to reproduction, we need not
delay to describe it more in detail.

To sum up briefly, "What is the secret of the
charm that this artist's works exercise upon an
ever-increasing multitude of admirers?" It lies
firstly in the vividly poetical imaginativeness of
his conceptions, and secondly in the wealth of
beautiful accessories in which he embodied and
enshrined them. He was not a great painter
in the true sense of the word. He never attained
to that absolute mastery of the materials of his
craft, that positively riotous ease of workmanship
that belonged to such painters as Rembrandt
and Velazquez, but among great artists he takes
his place undisputed in the very front rank. His
earlier work suffered technically from the delayed
commencement and peculiar nature of his art
education, and even in his maturer years, though
he attained a marvellous accuracy and exquisite-

ness of touch in drawing, he never reached rea
breadth or strength of style; but from the firs
he possessed an infallible sense of beauty o
form and colour, a powerful and overwhelming
originality, and an unequalled grace and delicacy
of fancy

CHRONOLOGICAL LIST OF CHIEF PICTURES

Picture.	*Owner.*
1860. Sidonia von Bork, and Clara von Bork.	*W. Graham Robertson, Esq.*
1861. The Enchantments of Nimue.	*Victoria and Albert Museum.*
1861. The Forge of Cupid.	*Mrs. R. H. Benson.*
1862. Fatima.	*The Earl of Carlisle.*
1863. Cinderella.	*A. E. Street, Esq.*
1863. St. Valentine's Morning.	*A. E. Street, Esq.*
1863. The Merciful Knight.	*John T. Middlemore, Esq.*
1865-72. Cupid and Psyche. Several versions painted.	
1865-6. St. George and the Dragon. (A set of seven pictures.)	*C. Sidney Goldmann.*
1866. St. Theophilus and the Angel.	*A. E. Street, Esq.*
1868-77. Le Chant d'amour.	*Mrs. Ismay.*

1869. The Wine of Circe.   *Miss Gertrude Foster.*

1869-71. Spring, with Summer, Autumn, Winter, Day and Night.
The first four, J. Douglas Fletcher, Esq. ; the last two, J. Ruston, Esq.

1869-79. Pygmalion and the Image.
(A set of four pictures.)
John T. Middlemore, Esq.

1869-98. The Prioress's Tale.   *Lady Colvile.*

1870. Love disguised as Reason.
Gertrude, Countess of Pembroke.

1870-83. The Hours.
Trustees of the late F. Austen, Esq.

1872. Temperantia.
Executors of the late Lord Wantage, V.C.

1872-76. The Angels of Creation.
(Six panels.)   *Alexander Henderson, Esq.*

1872-77. The Beguiling of Merlin.
Lilian, Duchess of Marlborough.

1872-81. The Feast of Peleus.
William Kenrick, Esq.

1873. Love among the Ruins.
Mrs. R. H. Benson.

1874-79. The Annunciation.
The Earl of Carlisle.

1876-80. The Golden Stairs.
The Lord Battersea.

1877. The Mirror of Venus.
                    C. Sidney Goldmann, Esq.
1877-83. The Wheel of Fortune.
        The Right Hon. Arthur J. Balfour, M.P.
1880. Dies Domini.   *The Earl of Carlisle.*
1881-82. The Tree of Forgiveness.
                            W. Imrie, Esq.
1883. King Cophetua and the
    Beggar-Maid.   *Tate Gallery.*
1883-93. Perseus and the Graiæ.
        The Right Hon. Arthur J. Balfour, M.P.
1884-90. The Rose Bower. (Set of
    four pictures, the Briar Rose.)
                    Alexander Henderson, Esq.
1886. Sibylla Delphica.   *Manchester Gallery.*
1886. The Depths of the Sea.
                    Mrs. R. H. Benson.
1886. Flamma Vestalis.   *The Lord Davey.*
1888. Danaë and the Brazen Tower.
                        Glasgow Gallery.
1891. The Star of Bethlehem.
                        Birmingham Gallery.
1893. Vespertina Quies.
                Mrs. Maurice Beddington.
1896. Aurora.   *Earl Cowper, K.G.*
    Arthur in Avalon. (Left unfinished.)
                    C. Sidney Goldmann, Esq.

LIST OF WORKS IN PUBLIC GALLERIES

BIRMINGHAM. CORPORATION ART GALLERIES.
  The Star of Bethlehem.
  Elijah.
  Mars.
  Numerous studies and cartoons.
LONDON. TATE GALLERY.
  King Cophetua and the Beggar-Maid.
LONDON. VICTORIA AND ALBERT MUSEUM.
  The Enchantments of Nimue.
  The Mill.
  Dorigen.
  The Tree of Life.
  Cassandra.
MANCHESTER. CORPORATION ART GALLERIES.
  Sibylla Delphica.
OXFORD. ASHMOLEAN MUSEUM.
  The Prioress's Tale (cabinet).
  Illustrations to Cupid and Psyche, and the
    Hill of Venus (pencil).
  Various studies.

74

A SHORT LIST OF PLACES WHERE WINDOWS BY BURNE-JONES MAY BE SEEN

Allerton.
Birmingham.
Bradford.
Brighouse.
Cambridge.
  Peterhouse, Jesus College, etc.
Dublin.
Dundee.
Edinburgh.
Easthampstead.
Greenock.
Kirkcaldy.
Liverpool.
London.
  Forest Hill.
  Fulham.
  Kentish Town.
  Marylebone.
  Putney.
  Savoy Chapel.
  Sloane Street.
  Vere Street.
  Victoria and Albert Museum.
  Whiteland's Training College.
Lyndhurst.
Marlborough College.
New Ferry.
Oxford.
  Christ Church, Brazenose.
Paisley.
Rochdale.
Rottingdean.
Salisbury.
Scarborough.
Tamworth.
Torquay.
Waltham Abbey.
Yarmouth.

CHISWICK PRESS : CHARLES WHITTINGHAM AND CO.
TOOKS COURT, CHANCERY LANE, LONDON.

The British Artists Series.

Large post 8vo, in special bindings, with 90 to 100 Illustrations, 7s. 6d. net each.

Sir Joshua Reynolds.

By LORD RONALD SUTHERLAND GOWER, F.S.A.

Sir Edward Burne-Jones, Bart.

By MALCOLM BELL.

Seventh Edition.

Sir J. E. Millais, Bart., P.R.A.

By A. LYS BALDRY.

Second Edition.

Frederic, Lord Leighton, P.R.A.

By ERNEST RHYS.

Fourth Edition.

The English Pre-Raphaelite Painters.

Their Associates and Successors.

By PERCY BATE.

Second Edition.

LONDON: GEORGE BELL & SONS.

I

Messrs. Bell's Books.

Great Masters in Painting and Sculpture.

Edited by G. C. WILLIAMSON, Litt.D.

Post 8vo, each with 40 illustrations and photogravure frontispiece. 5s. net.

BERNARDINO LUINI. By G. C. Williamson, Litt.D.
VELASQUEZ. By R. A. M. Stevenson.
ANDREA DEL SARTO. By H. Guinness.
LUCA SIGNORELLI. By Maud Cruttwell.
RAPHAEL. By H. Strachey.
CARLO CRIVELLI. By G. McNeil Rushforth, M.A.
CORREGGIO. By Selwyn Brinton, M.A.
DONATELLO. By Hope Rea.
PERUGINO. By G. C. Williamson, Litt.D.
SODOMA. By the Contessa Lorenzo Priuli-Bon.
DELLA ROBBIA. By the Marchesa Burlamacchi.
GIORGIONE. By Herbert Cook, M.A.
MEMLINC. By W. H. James Weale.
PIERO DELLA FRANCESCA. By W. G. Waters, M.A.
PINTORICCHIO. By Evelyn March Phillipps.
FRANCIA. By George C. Williamson, Litt.D.
BRUNELLESCHI. By Leader Scott.
MANTEGNA. By Maud Cruttwell.
REMBRANDT. By Malcolm Bell.
GIOTTO. By F. Mason Perkins.
WILKIE. By Lord Ronald Sutherland Gower, M.A., F.S.A.
GERARD DOU. By Dr. W. Martin.
WATTEAU. By Edgcumbe Staley, B.A.

In preparation :

EL GRECO. By Manuel B. Cossio, Litt.D., Ph.D.
TINTORETTO. By J. B. Stoughton Holborn, M.A.
BOTTICELLI. By A. Streeter.
LEONARDO DA VINCI. By Edward McCurdy, M.A.
PAOLO VERONESE. By Roger E. Fry.
GAUDENZIO FERRARI. By Ethel Halsey.

Others to follow.

Messrs. Bell's Books.

The Endymion Series.

Poems by Percy Bysshe Shelley.

ILLUSTRATED AND DECORATED BY R. ANNING BELL.
With Introduction by PROFESSOR WALTER RALEIGH.
Post 8vo, 7s. 6d.

Poems by John Keats.

ILLUSTRATED AND DECORATED BY R. ANNING BELL.
With Introduction by PROFESSOR WALTER RALEIGH.
Third Edition, post 8vo, 7s. 6d.

Poems by Robert Browning.

ILLUSTRATED AND DECORATED BY BYAM SHAW.
With Introduction by DR. R. GARNETT.
Second Edition, revised, post 8vo, 7s. 6d.

English Lyrics from Spenser to Milton.

ILLUSTRATED AND DECORATED BY R. ANNING BELL.
Selected with Introduction by JOHN DENNIS.
Post 8vo, 6s.

Milton's Minor Poems,
Including Comus and Samson Agonistes.

ILLUSTRATED AND DECORATED BY A. GARTH JONES.
Post 8vo, 6s.

The Poems of Edgar Allan Poe.

ILLUSTRATED AND DECORATED BY
W. HEATH ROBINSON.
With an Introduction by H. NOEL WILLIAMS.
Second Edition, post 8vo, 6s.

Bell's Cathedral Series.

Profusely Illustrated.

In specially designed cloth cover, crown 8vo,
1s. 6d. net each.

Now Ready.

BRISTOL.	NORWICH.
CANTERBURY.	OXFORD.
CARLISLE.	PETERBOROUGH.
CHESTER.	RIPON.
CHICHESTER.	ROCHESTER.
DURHAM.	ST. DAVID'S.
ELY.	ST. PAUL'S.
EXETER.	SALISBURY.
GLOUCESTER.	SOUTHWELL.
HEREFORD.	WELLS.
LICHFIELD.	WINCHESTER.
LINCOLN.	YORK.
MANCHESTER.	WORCESTER.

4

Bell's Cathedral Series—*continued.*

The following uniform Volumes are also published
1s. 6d. net each.

ENGLISH CATHEDRALS. An Itinerary and Description.

WESTMINSTER ABBEY.

ST. MARTIN'S CHURCH, CANTERBURY.

BEVERLEY MINSTER.

TEWKESBURY ABBEY AND DEERHURST PRIORY.

CHRISTCHURCH PRIORY AND WIMBORNE ABBEY.

BATH ABBEY, MALMESBURY ABBEY, AND BRADFORD-ON-AVON CHURCH.

STRATFORD-ON-AVON CHURCH.

Bell's Handbooks to Continental Churches.

Profusely Illustrated. Crown 8vo, 2s. 6d. net each.

CHARTRES: THE CATHEDRAL, and other Churches.

ROUEN: THE CATHEDRAL, and other Churches.

AMIENS: THE CATHEDRAL, and other Churches.

PARIS: NOTRE DAME.

MONT ST. MICHEL.

Life and Light Books.

Prettily Bound, 1s. net each.

1. THE GREATEST THING EVER KNOWN. By RALPH WALDO TRINE. 16*th Thousand.*

2. FATE MASTERED—DESTINY FULFILLED. By W. J. COLVILLE.

3. EVERY LIVING CREATURE. By RALPH WALDO TRINE.

4. LEGENDS AND LYRICS. By ADELAIDE A. PROCTER. 130*th Thousand.* First Series.

5. LEGENDS AND LYRICS. By ADELAIDE A. PROCTER. 99*th Thousand.* Second Series.

6. BILLY AND HANS: My Squirrel Friends. A True History. By W. J. STILLMAN.

7. KITH AND KIN: Poems of Animal Life selected by HENRY S. SALT.

8. CHARACTER-BUILDING: Thought Power. By RALPH WALDO TRINE.

9. LIGHT FROM THE EAST. Selections from the Teaching of the Buddha. By EDITH WARD.

10. PARABLES FROM NATURE. A Selection. By MRS. M. GATTY.

11. BETTER FOOD FOR BOYS. By EUSTACE H. MILES.

12. MATHEMATICAL LAW IN THE SPIRITUAL WORLD. By EUSTACE H. MILES.

13. MARCUS AURELIUS ANTONINUS. George Long's Translation.

14. AURORA LEIGH. By MRS. BROWNING.

15. TENNYSON'S IN MEMORIAM.

16. FRIENDS OF MINE. By MRS. CORBET SEYMOUR.

Messrs. Bell's Books.

Miniature Editions.

ILLUSTRATED BY ROBERT ANNING BELL.

*Printed in red and black at the Chiswick Press. In decorated
paper boards, 1s. 6d. net each; or in limp leather, 2s. 6d. net.*

Rubáiyát of Omar Khayyám.

RENDERED INTO ENGLISH VERSE BY
EDWARD FITZGERALD.

With 19 Illustrations.

The Odes of Keats.

With 21 Illustrations.

Keats' Isabella and the Eve of St. Agnes.

With 17 Illustrations.

Bell's Sonnets Series.

*Printed at the Chiswick Press, with borders and initials by
CHRISTOPHER DEAN. Royal 16mo, 2s. 6d. net each.*

THE SONNETS OF JOHN KEATS
THE SONNETS OF WILLIAM SHAKESPEARE.
SONNETS FROM THE PORTUGUESE. BY MRS.
BROWNING.
BROWNING'S RABBI BEN EZRA.
DANTE'S VITA NUOVA, OR NEW LIFE.
Newly translated by FRANCES DE MEŸ.
SONNETS BY WILLIAM WORDSWORTH.

7